Recession-Proof Income Cleaning Up in the Commercial Office Cleaning Business

Douglas A. Smith

Copyright © 2020 Douglas A. Smith
All rights reserved
First Edition

NEWMAN SPRINGS PUBLISHING
320 Broad Street
Red Bank, NJ 07701

First originally published by Newman Springs Publishing 2020

ISBN 978-1-64801-165-8 (Paperback)
ISBN 978-1-64801-166-5 (Digital)

Printed in the United States of America

I dedicate this book to my mother, Alene Campbell Smith, whose example instilled in me the value of education and hard work, and to Josephine Grant without whose love and kindness, I could not breathe.

Contents

I:	Foreword	7
II:	Introduction	9
III:	Where to Start?	13
	A. Choosing Your Market	13
	B. Market Research	14
IV:	Laying the Groundwork—A Foundation for Success	20
	C. Accounting (Keeping Track)	20
	D. Branding Your Business	24
	E. Legally Establishing Your Business	25
	F. Personnel—Building Your Labor Force	28
	G. Selecting the Necessary Tools and Equipment	30
V:	Finding Work	35
	H. Creating Advertising and Marketing Material	35
	I. Finding and Reaching Customers	40
VI:	Appendices	49
	J. Case Studies	49
VII:	Business Communication (Examples)	53
VIII:	Resource Guide	57

Foreword

If I had a crystal-ball I could not have predicted the current worldwide recession that has resulted from the COVID-19 pandemic or the prominent role that cleaning and disinfecting would take on in our daily lives. When I sat down to write Recession Proof Income in the summer of 2017 my goal was to write a book that would help people earn a decent income in both good and bad economic times by establishing a commercial office cleaning business.

When I submitted my book to the publisher for consideration, it did not include a Foreword. The Foreword was added just as the book was heading for final publication. I felt it was necessary given that we are in the midst of a global pandemic that has killed thousands and has left many millions unemployed.

I wanted to assure the public that I am not an opportunist seeking to capitalize on this global crisis. Seeking to profit from such human suffering is amoral and contrary to my spiritual beliefs. I completed my book in early 2019 and signed a contract with my publisher in November that same year. It has taken nearly a year for the book to go through editing, typesetting, cover design, printing, marketing, etc. The publication and release of the book at this time is a mere coincidence.

It would be dishonest of me to deny that I recognize this pandemic has created a changing point for the commercial office cleaning business. It has produced a worldwide demand for individuals and companies that provide those services and has provided a tremendous opportunity to earn big profits.

However, I believe it will be important to the success of a person just starting out in the commercial office cleaning business to remember that this opportunity is not just about money and profits.

This business had become essential, if not critical to man's physical health and overall survival. We should be humbled that this pandemic and the resulting demand for our services gives those of us involved in this industry the unique opportunity to directly affect the wellbeing of all humanity.

Good luck in this endeavor and Godspeed.

Douglas A. Smith
June 4th, 2020

Introduction

In the mid-1990s, I was reintroduced to the commercial office cleaning business. I say *reintroduced* because when I was a teenager, growing up in rural West Virginia, I had a part-time job, cleaning doctor's offices in the evening, while my best friend had a job cleaning a barbershop. The money wasn't great, just enough to keep us up to date with the latest records and other teenage junk. Little did I know then, that as I got older and more educated, I would revert back to this teenage occupation as my primary means of earning a *good* adult living.

While working as a purchasing agent for a major Washington DC building contractor, I met this guy who worked in my building. A quiet and unassuming person, he worked in the mail room for another company within the building. However, every evening, after leaving his day job, he would go and clean a small private school in suburban Virginia. One day, we were standing in front of the building, taking a break and talking. He began to tell me a story about a guy, who during the Great Depression drove a new Cadillac every year, wore expensive suits, and smoked fat cigars.

While others were jumping out of windows, riding the rails, and eating at soup kitchens, this guy was enjoying the good life. How did he do it? What did he know that those suffering did not? They say that most truths are simple. Well, this guy's truth was no different. He realized that no matter how *good or bad* the world's economy was doing, with few exceptions, the people who work all day in an office building or other businesses are not going to stay and clean them at night.

This simple truth remains a fact today, just the same as it did nearly a century ago. No matter the upturns or downturns in the economy, the opportunity to earn a good living by providing this basic but highly necessary service will remain for the foreseeable future.

I listened as this guy spoke, and I took it all in and kept it in the back of my mind. Well, a few years later when I got tired of working for someone else, I began to look around for opportunity. I thought about selling real estate, cars, etc. After a long while, I began to realize that the best thing I had to sell was my labor. The work I was trained to do offered lots of opportunity to earn a living, but it wasn't recession proof. Any downturn in the construction industry could leave me in a precarious financial situation.

One day while meditating on the problem, I remembered my conversation from years earlier with the guy who worked in my building. As I began to seriously consider the idea of starting my own commercial office cleaning business, I quickly became overwhelmed. Where would I start? How would I start? Would I quit my job? What tools and equipment would I need? Where would I find jobs? How much money did I need to get started? Unfortunately, there were no books available on how to start a commercial office cleaning company.

Drawing upon my education, business experience, and after much trial and error, I was able to start my own company. Soon, I started to pick-up jobs and began to earn a steady income. With repeat customers and a steady flow of new one-time customers, I was soon earning more money than I ever earned working for someone else. After about three years, I was earning in excess of $100,000 a year, and after about seven years, I sold my business for a nice sum of money.

Fortunately, you do not have go through the trial and error that I did in order to start your very own commercial office cleaning business. In this book, I have laid out concrete steps, detailing everything you will need to do to get up and running quickly without a complicated business plan, and more importantly, without breaking the bank.

Filled with suggestions from real-world business experience, this book will show you exactly how to start your business. We will show

RECESSION PROOF INCOME CLEANING UP IN THE COMMERCIAL OFFICE CLEANING BUSINESS

you how to choose your market, lay the groundwork for a successful business, and most importantly, how to find customers and begin reaping profits. So buckle up, sit back, and enjoy the ride because you are now on your way to cleaning up in the commercial office cleaning business. I wish you every success in your new venture.

Douglas A. Smith

Where to Start?

All things we endeavor to accomplish in life require a starting point. Business is no different. People wishing to start a business are often unsure of exactly where to begin and, sometimes, waste valuable time and resources by starting at an inappropriate point.

This is easy to understand because many books written about starting a business differ in their approach, and much of the time, these books end up overwhelming and paralyzing the potential businessowner. They usually find their way to the bookshelf or the trash heap, having failed in helping the person get started in business.

The simple, yet prudent, approach I took in starting my business is highlighted in the section below. I believe it to be both a practical and logical place in which to start a commercial office cleaning business.

Choosing Your Market

Knowing and deciding what type of cleaning business to start can be a little overwhelming. Like most businesses, the commercial office cleaning and janitorial business is complex and spans across multiple market segments. Each one, offering its own risk and benefits, from dangerous working conditions to enormous profits.

Highlighted below are some of the more common office cleaning/janitorial market segments for you to examine before choosing your market and starting your business. They range from the simple to the complex and vary in the amount of resources needed to start up. You may consider providing services across all market segments or may already have a particular segment in mind. You may even choose a mix of market segments in order to generate revenue from multiple sources. The choice is yours.

1. Commercial Office Cleaning/Janitorial Services
    a) Doctors' offices—large/small practices
    b) Law offices—large/small
    c) Industrial offices—administrative offices of warehouses, etc.
    d) Barbershops and beauty salons
    e) Private schools and day cares
    f) Restaurants
2. Construction and Specialized Cleaning Services
    a) Construction trailers
    b) Site preparation—debris removal
    c) Day porters
    d) Final cleaning
    e) Stripping and waxing floors
    f) Bronze (metal) polishing
    g) Windows (high-rise and storefronts)
    h) Building graffiti removal
3. Personal (Home/Maid) Services
    a) Private homes (single family)
    b) Condos
    c) College fraternity/sorority houses
    d) Special events

Market Research

It takes a tremendous amount of financial and human capital to start and grow a business of any kind. Therefore, prudent business practices would dictate that before starting your business, a proper study of your industry (market research) should be conducted and careful consideration given to the amount of capital necessary to achieve market penetration and to successfully compete.

The amount of effort spent performing market research will directly relate to how successful your business will be in the actual marketplace. Your research should be as far-reaching and in-depth

RECESSION PROOF INCOME CLEANING UP IN THE COMMERCIAL OFFICE CLEANING BUSINESS

as time and money will allow. No matter how in-depth you decide your research should go, of paramount importance is that your market research answers these three fundamental questions: (1) Does the market exist? (2) What are the market and conditions? and (3) What are the potential barriers to successful market entry?

1. Does the Market Exist?

Does the market exist for your services? Today, there is a large number of business development incubators, university programs, and independent firms that can assist you in conducting the necessary market research to make this determination. However, if you are like me, you neither have the time nor financial resources necessary to conduct a thorough and comprehensive research study of the cleaning/janitorial business.

Relying upon my education, business experience, and the many public library resources available at the time (no internet), I was able to gather a large amount of data on the subject, synthesize it, and conduct my own "common sense market research."

To over simplify, my research concluded that (1) human beings are messy; (2) wherever there are humans, there will always be dirt; (3) humans and dirt cannot healthfully coexist for extended periods; (4) despite the nature of dirt, not all humans will clean; and (5) some segments of the human population will always require assistance in meeting their cleaning needs.

Although I have oversimplified and took some levity with the market research I conducted, my fundamental goal was to determine (1) if the market existed; and (2) was there a stable demand for my services both now and in the future. With my preliminary market research concluded and the results in hand, I decided that there was an existing market for my services and that the market would remain stable for the foreseeable future.

2. What Are the Market Conditions?

As a kid, before we jumped into the pool on a hot summer day, we dipped our foot into the water to gauge the temperature. If it was too cold, we would sit on the side with our feet in the water, and only after becoming acclimated, did we jump in. That is, if the pool wasn't too crowded. That process is exactly what you are doing when you begin to analyze the conditions of your chosen market. Two important areas for consideration are market size and competition.

Determine the size of your market. You will want to know who your potential customers are—that is, who has a demand for your services? For instance, if you chose to focus your business on construction final cleaning, you would need to know *who* (building contractors) and *how many* are doing business in your market's service area. Conducting a simple internet search should suffice in identifying your potential customers. If not, check with your local or state agency responsible for issuing business licenses.

The next steps would be to determine that out of the total number of potential customers, how many have ongoing or upcoming projects that currently need or will need your services; and of those, how many have existing relationships with your competitors, or are they accepting new bidders on projects? Call, text, email, or write a letter to find out this much-needed information. As you begin to answer these questions, you will be able to determine if your market is growing, stagnant, or in decline; who your competitors are; and if the market is too saturated to obtain a market share sufficient to produce your desired profits.

Knowing who your competitors are and how saturated the market begins with identifying *who* (cleaning/janitorial companies) and *how many* are doing business in your market's service area. Conducting a simple internet search should suffice in identifying your competitors. If not, check with your local or state agency responsible for issuing business licenses, or perhaps, utilize the best method of all, talk to your potential customers and find out who is currently fulfilling their service needs.

RECESSION PROOF INCOME CLEANING UP IN THE COMMERCIAL OFFICE CLEANING BUSINESS

Learning as much information as you can about your competitors' business operations should be your primary goal. Your research should ask questions, such as how many employees do your competitors have and how many do they utilize on their various sized projects; what types of equipment do they use and what condition are they in; what is their approach to marketing; and how do they price their services. Knowing the answer to these and other pertinent questions will help you to focus your efforts and tailor a marketing approach that diminishes your competitors' strengths and exploits their weaknesses.

3. What Are the Market Barriers?

Making entry into an existing business market can be as daunting as scaling the Empire State Building with a ladder. That is not to say that insurmountable obstacles cannot be conquered. My business experiences prove that they can. Commitment, drive, diligent effort, and applied intelligence make market penetration and business success obtainable. Although, they can be formidable, three of the most common market barriers are legal/regulatory requirements, market knowledge, and financial resources.

a. *Legal/regulatory requirements.* Depending on which market segment you choose to concentrate your business, proper consideration should be given to the legal/regulatory requirements, which could present a host of challenges to your new business.

For instance, in choosing to provide cleaning services to schools or government facilities, you and your employees may have to undergo personal background checks and provide police clearances at your own expense. The government may require your business to have special licenses and carry expensive liability insurance just to enter their facility.

In addition, local, state, and federal environmental regulations may require you to provide material safety data sheets (MSDS) for the chemicals used in cleaning and provide for the safe storage, use, and disposal of said chemicals. Further regulations could require your company to recycle all plastic and paper waste products collected from your facilities.

As you see, the legal/regulatory requirements can be quite extensive and present real challenges for the new business. The key is to identify them before attempting market entry and plan accordingly.

b. *Market knowledge.* It should go without saying that as a businessowner, you should have in-depth knowledge of the market you are in. However, you would be surprised at the number of businessowners who know little about their market's demands and particular nuances their clients expect them to understand. This is often reflected in the business proposal or bid submitted to the owner or contracting officer of the potential client.

New business owners sometime submit written proposals for services not associated to the potential client's industry. For instance, they will submit a janitorial proposal for a construction final cleaning project. This is a red flag that signals the potential client that this business does not understand their business needs and therefore select another proposal.

To avoid making this mistake, businessowners must take the time to understand exactly what business they are in. To educate themselves, owners should talk to industry professionals, read industry-trade publications, and should the market dictate, take formal classes. Understanding the specific needs of your industry will help eliminate this market barrier and position your business as a company in the know, a company who understands and can fulfill their customers' needs.

c. *Financial resources.* Money, money, money. The depth of your company's financial resources can determine whether market entry can be achieved. The demand for specific cleaning equipment, staff demands, insurance requirements, bonds, etc., can all be factors that hinder successful entry. Start as small or as big as your resources will allow; however, a watchful eye on expenses is always prudent.

As a new business, it may be wise to start small until you know exactly what you've gotten yourself into. For instance, should you choose to enter the construction final cleaning market, you do not have to chase the million-square-foot project, the fifteen-hundred-

RECESSION PROOF INCOME CLEANING UP IN THE
COMMERCIAL OFFICE CLEANING BUSINESS

square-foot retail space will do. This will allow you to get to know your industry while managing your financial resources and maximizing their use.

Laying the Groundwork—A Foundation for Success

You have conducted your research, selected your market, and are now ready to start your business. To increase your likelihood of success, we suggest you start your business on a firm foundation. In this section we introduce and discuss some fundamental business concepts that will help you in accomplishing that task. Some of these concepts may be familiar, while others are completely new. They are presented in the order we think they should be undertaken and in accordance with our own real-world experience.

Accounting (Keeping Track)

Most books on starting a business will begin with having you choose your business structure (corporation, sole proprietor, partnership, etc.). However, long before you get to that point, you have already committed and expended valuable resources toward starting your business. Some of which, under current IRS rules, may be deductible as business expenses.

Fundamental to the success of any business enterprise is its ability to keep track of and manage expenses. In order to track your start-up and ongoing business expenses, you will need to either (a) hire an accountant; (b) purchase and install accounting software on your computer; or (c) set up a simple (T-Account) bookkeeping system. Each of these options have their advantages, however, no matter which option you choose, the fundamental point is that you have, from the beginning, a system in place to keep track of all the expenses related to your business operations.

RECESSION PROOF INCOME CLEANING UP IN THE COMMERCIAL OFFICE CLEANING BUSINESS

The following section provides a brief discussion of each of the above options; however, please note the one you choose should take in consideration your knowledge of accounting practices and procedures and the amount of money you have to spend. Whichever option you choose, remember that keeping track is the fundamental business concept because no matter how recession-proof your income, if you do not keep track and manage your business expenses, you may soon find your business in financial ruin.

a)   Hiring an Accountant

At some point, every business will need to hire an accountant because of taxes. However, when you are first starting out, it is entirely up to you whether you do or don't. The determining factor will depend on your knowledge of accounting, your planned business structure, and the amount of money you have to procure the services of an accountant. Should you have the financial resources to hire an accountant, please consider the following before making your choice:

Is the person or firm you are considering a licensed professional, a certified public accountant (CPA), or are they simply a bookkeeper? A CPA is licensed by the state and held to a higher standard of professional responsibility than a person who is simply a bookkeeper. The CPA has likely passed a criminal background check; whereas, a criminal background check of a bookkeeper will depend entirely on your own due diligence. Who you want watching your money is entirely up to you, but the prudent business decision would be to hire the CPA.

The level of accounting services required. A bookkeeper can set up your ledgers and keep track of your income and expenses. They may even be able to provide monthly statements, yet they are usually limited as to the services they can provide either by law, education, or training. A CPA can provide a full range of accounting services, from simple bookkeeping, monthly statements, managerial advice, to tax planning. In addition, a CPA may be able to help you choose a business structure that allows your business to take maximum advantage of current tax laws and can help to register your company with the proper state authorities.

b) Purchasing and Installing Software

Assuming that you have knowledge of basic accounting practices and procedures, you may elect to purchase an accounting software package and install it on your home/office computer. It is not within the scope of this book to evaluate and recommend specific accounting software. Some available software includes Sage 50c Accounting, QuickBooks Premier, Xerox, FreshBooks, and QuickBooks Online. A Google search on these products will provide a starting point for your evaluation. It is important that your selection be carefully evaluated and your decision based on your projected needs. When making your selection, please keep in mind these key factors.

The software should have industry-specific (janitorial/custodial) templates that will aid in setting up your ledgers. Some software programs on the market have built-in capabilities designed for the janitorial/custodial industry. It will automatically setup accounts for cleaning supplies, equipment purchases, etc.

Is the software capable of tracking and reporting project- or job-specific income/expenses? Every dollar earned and expense related to a job should be recorded and charged to that job. Keeping track of a particular job's or project's profit or loss will be essential to the success of your business.

c) Setting-Up T-Accounts

T-accounts are a simplified way of keeping track of business-related income and expenses. When you are just starting your business, it is a great way of keeping track without getting weighted down with the many dynamics of business accounting. This is a simple and easy way of keeping track, but please remember, at some point, *you will* have to invest in accounting software and/or the services of an accountant. It is not a bad idea to take a couple of accounting courses

RECESSION PROOF INCOME CLEANING UP IN THE COMMERCIAL OFFICE CLEANING BUSINESS

at your local community college or online, just so you will be able to keep up with your business's basic accounting needs.

T-accounts get their name from the shape of the account. In their simplest form, the left side of the T is reserved for debits (expenses) and the right side of the T is reserved for credits (cash, prepaid expenses, etc.). The example below shows how to setup a basic T-account.

Office Supplies

	Debits	Credits
Printer Ink	$60	
Copy Paper	$7	
Staples	$5	
Total	**$72.00**	

Cleaning Equipment

	Debits	Credits
Vacuum	$140	
Buffer	$250	
P. Washer	$350	
Total	**$740.00**	

Cleaning Supplies

	Debits	Credits
Detergents	$50	
Sponges	$10	
Cleaning Rags	$6	
Total	**$66.00**	

Cash Account

	Debits	Credits
		$5,000
Office Supplies	$72	$4,928
Cleaning Equip.	$740	$4,188
Cleaning Supplies	$66	$4,122
Total	**$878**	**$4,122**

From the example above, let us say that you expended $72 for office supplies, $740 for cleaning equipment, and $66 for cleaning supplies. Each of these cash expenditures were offset against the

$5,000 cash account and reflect an ending cash balance after expenses of $4,122. As you can see, T-accounts are a simple but effective method of keeping track of business-related income and expenses.

For your business, you would have to setup accounts for each type of business-related income and expense, such as office supplies, equipment, materials, gas, labor, legal services, accounting services, checking accounts, petty cash, etc. Please don't forget that in addition to setting up T-accounts to track overall business income and expenses, you will have to do this on a job or project basis as well. This will enable you keep an eye on the bottom line, job by job.

Branding Your Business

When choosing a name, logo, and slogan for your company, you are essentially creating a market brand. A good business name, identifiable logo, and memorable slogan are valuable commodities, yet many small businessowners approach the branding process with cavalier or clever simplicity instead of treating it like an important business strategy and valuable asset. How potential customers associate a business with the services it provides is an important factor in determining whether a company will be successful.

1. Choosing a Business Name

A good company name will reflect your business's market concentration and have broad market appeal. Example, Sam's Office Cleaning Service tells potential customers that you provide cleaning services to offices. The business name can also be very specific such as Sam's Doctor's Office Cleaning Service. This would be great if Sam's business was solely concentrated on doctor's offices.

Be careful not to pigeonhole your company. A better name would reflect the company's market concentration without locking it into a limited market, such as Sam's Commercial Office Cleaning Services. A perfect example of this concept is IBM—International Business Machines—the all-encompassing name speaks for itself.

2. Creating a Graphic Representation (Logo)

Designing or choosing a graphic representation (logo) for your company should involve the same level of strategic planning as selecting your name. An image is worth a thousand words. People often associate an image with a company and the services it provides. A man dressed in a service uniform, holding a mop and bucket, would be an excellent representation for a janitorial company. When choosing a logo, think McDonalds' golden arches.

3. Developing a Business Slogan

Just as when choosing a name and designing a logo, careful thought should go into developing a company slogan. A good slogan can speak volumes about a company and provide an edge over the competition. A good slogan is catchy, easy to remember, and provides an outstanding representation of what your company is all about. For instance, Coke Cola, the real thing, suggest that all other colas are unreal and theirs is better simply because it is the "real thing." Which would you buy?

Legally Establishing Your Business

Once you have chosen a name for your business, it is a good idea to register the name with your state and secure a taxpayer or employer identification number (TIN or EIN) from the United States Internal Revenue Service. Deciding on the legal structure for your business is of the utmost importance. Because of the legal and tax ramification of your decision, it is prudent to consult a lawyer.

There are several publications on the market, and in some states, the office of the Secretary of State sanction or hosts websites that explain each of the legal forms your business can take and the process and procedures for establishing each one. It is not within the scope or the intent of this book to give legal advice. The following is a brief overview of the most common business forms and some of their key features.

1. Sole Proprietorships

Perhaps one of the most common and easiest business forms to establish, the sole proprietorship is identified by these key features:

The business is owned and managed by one person.

Sole proprietor retains all profits and bears all losses.

Sole proprietor's personal assets can be reached to satisfy business obligations (i.e., personal liability).

2. General Partnerships

Establishing this business form normally requires the assistance of an attorney because most states require that partnership agreements be filed with the state in order to form the business and, once formed, require formal notice in order to dissolve the partnership.

Formed by agreements, either oral or written.

All partners share rights to manage the partnership.

Partners share profits and losses according to their agreement; if no agreement, profits and losses are shared equally, regardless of capital contributions.

Partners have unlimited personal liability for partnership obligations.

Liability is joint and several—meaning that any partner—is completely liable for any debt.

Easily and inexpensively formed.

Partners owe each other fiduciary duties. Partners can transfer their partnership interest, but transferee becomes a partner only upon consent of other partners.

Withdrawal of a partner may not necessarily cause a dissolution and winding up of the partnership; in many instances, the dissociating partner is bought out.

3. Limited Liability Partnerships (LLP)

As the name indicates, the main feature of the LLP is to limit the liability of each individual partner and the business as a whole. The following are some of the LLP's key features.

Partners in LLPs have no liability in any state for wrongful acts of their copartners.

In thirty-six states, LLP partners have no liability, either for wrongful acts of their copartners or for contractual obligations of the partnership.

Partners in LLPs retain liability for their won wrongful acts and those they direct or supervise.

LLPs can be formed only by complying with state statutes that require the filling of any application with the appropriate state agency.

The LLP agreement may be oral or written; in the absence of an agreement, profits, losses, management, and control are shared equally regardless of capital contributions.

Some states require the LLP to carry insurance or meet financial responsibility standards.

Not every dissociation cause a termination and winding up; in many instances, a dissociating member's interest will be purchased.

LLPs have the pass-through taxation of general partnerships.

4. Limited Liability Companies (LLC)

Sometimes called a limited liability corporation, LLCs serve to limit the liability of the business's member owners, provides certain tax advantages, and protects their personal assets.

LLCs offer their members full protection from personal liability.

LLCs can be managed by their members (member-managed) or by appointed managers (manager-managed).

LLCs can be formed only by compliance with state statues, which mandate the filing of articles of organization with the state agency.

The LLC is governed by its operating agreement, which is usually written. If the operating agreement is silent on various matters, the pertinent state LLC statute will control.

Unless the operating agreement provides otherwise, admission of a new member usually required unanimous approval.

The LLC provides the pass-through taxation of a general partnership.

5. Corporations

Corporations are both simple and complex. They exist in many different forms, and their rights and responsibilities are numerous. Their formation, finances, management, profits, dividends, and regulation are the subject of many business school texts; however, we will confine our discussion to the basic features of this most dynamic and unique business form.

Corporations are persons and exist separate and apart from their owner-shareholders.

Offer limited liability for their shareholders, officers, directors because the corporation itself is liable for its own debts and obligations.

Can exist perpetually.

Ownership is easily transferred.

Corporations are subject to double taxation; the income of a corporation is taxed, and when profits are distributed to shareholders, they also pay tax on the money received.

Can be expensive to form and maintain.

Management of corporations is centralized in a board of directors; the owner-shareholders do not manage the typical large business corporation.

Personnel—Building Your Labor Force

Being self-motivated and independent are essential personality traits of the successful businessowner. However, those very traits can lead a business to failure. How? Simply put, no person can do it all. We all need help, dividing the labor responsibilities and putting the right team together is as an important business decision as any other decision previously discussed.

When I first started my cleaning business, it was only me. I did everything, drafting marketing material, making sales calls, performing the work, etc. As the volume of work increased, I quickly realized I could not do it all. Panic set in. I couldn't afford to hire anyone to help me, neither did I trust anyone to perform the work to my standards. What was I to do? My brand was at stake. To get a handle on the situation, I had to stop panicking and take a systematic approach to my problem. These are the steps that I took.

1. Strengths and Weaknesses

First, I made an assessment of my individual strengths and weaknesses to determine where they would help or hurt my business.

I listed the areas of the business where my strengths should be focused, i.e., marketing, sales, management.

Then I listed the areas of the business where I needed support because of my weaknesses, i.e., performing the work, technical knowledge, direct employee supervision.

2. Personnel Wanted (Type, Quality, Quantity)

Next, I made an assessment of the type, quality, and quantity of the personnel needed, which would compensate for my weak areas and help me develop and grow my business.

The type of personnel I needed was those who had basic knowledge of commercial office cleaning and possessed some technical knowledge—i.e., dusting the high areas (ceiling fans, bookshelves, etc.), before dusting the low areas (desk, computers, etc.).

A commercial office cleaning operation has to employ and meet the standards required by the customer; therefore, I needed personnel who possessed a mature and responsible work ethic and who were honest and trustworthy.

At the beginning of my business, I had few contracts that required more than one or two people. As the business began to grow, and cleaning contracts became larger and more diverse, I needed to increase the number of personnel.

Finally, to ensure I found and assembled the right team, I wrote job descriptions and outlined responsibilities for each permanent and temporary position created.

3. Assembling the Team

Finally, with all the information gleamed from my assessments, I set out to build my team.

Low lying fruit. I looked at family, friends, and casual acquaintances that possessed knowledge of the office cleaning business, had the technical skills, and had the requisite qualities I needed.

I identified temporary employment companies who could supply the needed personnel on demand, within short notice and at a reasonable rate.

I reached out to local community organizations, i.e., churches, missions, etc., to identify potential workers.

After taking these steps, I was able to identify an old acquaintance that had knowledge of the industry, technical knowledge (stripping and waxing floors, cleaning compounds, equipment, etc.), and who possessed the qualities I was looking for in an employee. He became my operations manager who aided in selecting and supervising our cleaning teams, to ensure conformity with the written job descriptions and the demands of the particular cleaning contract.

Selecting the Necessary Tools and Equipment

Despite what market segment you decide to enter, you will need a wide variety of cleaning materials, janitorial supplies, tools, and equipment. You will need tools and equipment that will allow you to clean high, low, and in-between. Your equipment should be efficient and reliable, and most importantly, designed for the job at hand.

RECESSION PROOF INCOME CLEANING UP IN THE COMMERCIAL OFFICE CLEANING BUSINESS

The list below is a compilation of the most common tools and equipment used in the cleaning/janitorial business. It is best to start your business with new items from the list; however, when I first started, I used many of the items from my home closet. Most of the items on the list can be purchased for minimal cost from Home Depot or Lowes.

However, if possible, it would be better to purchase your inventory from a local janitorial supply company who has industry related equipment designed for the services you will likely perform, specialized knowledge of cleaning compounds and techniques, and the ability to offer credit and discounts on items purchases. The earlier you start a relationship with a reliable supplier, the better your opportunity for success, because suppliers are a valuable resource to your business and essential to your growth.

The following is a basic list of items you will need to get started. This list should not be considered all-inclusive as some cleaning projects will require specialized equipment and/or cleaning compounds. If you are unsure about what you will need for the type of project you are working on, consult your supplier.

Floors

- Vacuums (portable)
- Cloth mops
- Dust mops
- Mop buckets w/ringers
- Buffer w/pads (stripping/waxing)
- Brooms (straw, nylon, and push)
- Signage (wet floor, danger)

Surfaces

- Cloth cleaning rags
- Sponges and squeegees
- Nonabrasive cleaning pads
- Feather dusters (short/long reach)

Cleaning/Janitorial Supplies

    Liquid soap (floors)
    Liquid soap (hand dispensers)
    Bleach
    Ammonia
    Deodorizers
    Glass cleaner
    Stainless steel polish
    Brass polish
    Paper towels
    Trash bags
    Tissue products (toilet, hand towels, etc.)

PRICING YOUR SERVICES

How you determine the value of your services is probably one of biggest factors in whether your business succeeds or fails. Some cleaning businesses price their services based on the total square footage of the space to be cleaned. Some calculate their price by the unit cost of such items as estimated man hours, materials needed, travel distance, etc. Others use a combination of methods in determining price while many price their services according to whatever the market will bear.

Whatever method you choose the bottom line is to make a profit. Hopefully, during your market research you uncovered the answer to this question and have decided on the best practice for your particular market. However, there are certain to be projects that you overprice and some that you under price. If you are keeping track, i.e. accounting cost by project, these miscalculations will be a wealth of knowledge for the future health of your business.

Independent of the market segment you choose to focus your business, the following questions should be answered when deciding price? Who, What, When, Where, and How?

Who is the client and what are their expectations and demands? For example, when I first started in business, I had a lot of barber shops whose owners demanded that the tile floors be kept immaculate and expected them to always shine like new money. This meant that I had to ensure that all the cut hair was swept clean, the floors mopped, waxed, buffed, and occasionally stripped, re-waxed and buffed. Because of who the clients were, (barber shops) and their expectations and demands (specialized floor treatment), I was able to charge a premium price over and above the price for just plain cleaning services.

What resources will you have to bring to bear in order to perform the service? What cleaning supplies and equipment will you need? What human resources will you need? Ex. hand soap and tissue for the bathrooms, floor soap, wax, bleach, glass cleaner for the mirrors, brooms, mops, buckets, floor buffer, pads, etc.

When will you have to provide the service? Will service be required one or more times a week, during the day, at night, the weekend, holidays, etc.

Where will the service be required? This question sounds too obvious, but the service location of the business must be considered when determining price because of expenses related to travel such as gas, time, and vehicle wear and tear.

Perhaps the most important question in determining the price for your company's services, is the question of **How**? How can you provide the service that meets the customer's expectations and demands, does not create a strain on resources, and produces a profit? And most importantly, how can you provide the service at a price the customer agrees to pay?

Finding Work

You have chosen your market and have laid a strong foundation for your business success. Now, you are ready to go out and start making money, but where and how will you start? One of the biggest challenges you will face as a businessowner will be how do you find, attract, and keep a steady flow of customers. There have been many books written on the subject of marketing and sales techniques. Those books talk about the four p(s)—product placement, market positioning, promotion, and price; in addition to specific sales techniques, such as door-to-door sales.

Planning and implementing an effective marketing and sales program will be imperative to your business success; therefore, it would not be a waste of you time or resources to conduct an in-depth study of these subjects. However, the purpose of this book is to help get your business up and running quickly. In this section, we have outlined some simple, yet proven, steps you can take to start attracting customers and earning profits immediately.

Creating Advertising and Marketing Material

If you are going to spend valuable resources on your business, i.e., money; this is the one area where you should go all out and avoid cutting corners. When meeting potential customers, it is important you have in hand a brochure, business card, or some other material that introduces your company. Your advertising and marketing material is the first opportunity you have to make a good impression on potential customers.

In section 3, Laying the Groundwork., we briefly discussed business branding. This is where the time and effort you put into developing your brand comes into play. The name you have chosen for your business, your logo, and your business slogan should be incorporated into any advertising brochures, business cards, flyers, etc., that you develop. Below is a list of suggestions that will be helpful in developing your material.

1. Brochures (Trifold)

We recommend that you create some simple trifold brochures to distribute to potential customers. This can be done utilizing the services of a professional or can be created on a desktop using Microsoft Word or other commercially available software program.

Your brochure design should include your company name, logo, and slogan. In addition, your physical address, phone, email, website, etc., should be prominent on the front and rear of the brochure. All information should be presented in reasonably big and bold copy so it will jump out and catch the eye of potential customers.

The use of different fonts as well as bold and italic formats is highly effective in bringing attention to your brochure, particularly when quoting your company slogan. Please keep in mind that that same design should be used across all platforms employed in advertising and marketing your business, i.e., business cards, flyers, website, etc.

The use of color is highly recommended; however, whatever colors you choose, please keep in mind the colors should not distract your customers from your message or provoke a negative emotion in your potential customer. We recommend you familiarize yourself with the ample research available on the topic of using color to persuade.

Write clear and concise paragraphs that conveys the who, what, when, where, why, and how of your business.

Who. Your brochure should tell potential customers more than just your name. For instance, "We are a full-service janitorial company certified and endorsed by the US Association of Building Owners and dedicated to providing quality professional and reliable service in keeping with industry standards."

RECESSION PROOF INCOME CLEANING UP IN THE COMMERCIAL OFFICE CLEANING BUSINESS

What. Tell your potential customers what services you offer, i.e., weekly maid service, clean-up after special events, etc. Services can be efficiently conveyed utilizing bold bullet points in the layout. Example:

* *Maid Service*
* *Special Events*
* *Day Porters*

When. Your potential customers will want to know how flexible your company is in providing it service offerings. Let them know if you are available weekends, afterhours, on short notice, etc.

Where. Tell potential customers in what geographic areas your services are available, i.e., citywide, nationwide, county, state, metro area, etc.

Why. This is where you get to do some modest bragging. Tell potential customers why they should use your service over the competition. Highlight any specialized processes, techniques, or capabilities that separate your company from any other. Before and after pictures can be highly effective in this area.

How. Very important that your potential customers know all the ways they can contact your company, i.e., phone, fax, email, website, etc.

2. Business Cards

A business card can be an inexpensive and highly cost-effective method of reaching potential customers. Attendance at networking and industry-related events are the perfect opportunities to pass out cards. In addition, meeting someone for the first time while standing in line at the grocery store, Home Depot, or the DMV provide unexpected opportunities to reach potential customers. Below are some basic things to consider regarding the use of business cards.

Like your brochure, the design of your business card should include your business name, logo, and slogan. The design elements, fonts, colors, letter styles of your card should mirror those of your brochure wherever possible.

Be sure to include your physical address, phone, email, website, etc.

Titles such as owner, director of sales and marketing, customer service, etc., should be indicated on your business card. Potential customers like to know to whom they are talking. They will want to know if you are a decision maker and someone they can contact for their business needs.

A business card should be kept with you at all times because you never know when you may meet a potential customer.

3. Business Flyers

Business flyers can be an inexpensive and effective method for attracting potential customers. They can be distributed at industry events, business opportunity conferences, etc. Here are some hard and fast rules concerning the use of business flyers.

Like your brochure and business cards, the design of your business flyers should include your business name, logo, and slogan. The design elements, fonts, colors, letter styles of your flyers should mirror those of your brochure and cards wherever possible.

Never, ever, put business flyers on cars at malls, shopping centers, etc. It only serves to anger people and has the potential to drive away customers.

Do not put flyers in potential customers' mailboxes. It is illegal. However, reaching potential customers through a direct mail campaign can be highly effective, provided you have the capital.

Business flyers should be kept with you at all times. As business flyers are less expensive to produce than brochures, they can be handed out to potential customers. And the more expensive brochures can be reserved for strong leads or potential customers you may want to impress.

4. Business Website

In the days before the internet, a company could choose a name like A-1 Janitorial and secure top of the page listing in the yellow pages. With a large ad the company was more likely to be seen and selected before any other company on the page. It is no different in today's marketplace. Internet search engines play an important role in determining what company gets top billing.

Today's business climate dictates your business has a presence on the World Wide Web. Having a presence on the "web" provides certain advantages for the well-positioned and technology-savvy business. Not only can a website provide a convenient and cost-efficient method for distributing information about your business services, it can provide a platform for handling customer request, complaints, scheduling projects, ordering supplies, paying vendors, receiving payments, and a host of other services.

It is not within the scope of this book to tell you how to build a website or how to optimize your company's profile. We suggest you consult with a qualified website developer. At the start of your business, it may not be cost-efficient for your business to develop a website. No worries, you can still attract customers. You will just have to use more conventional or old-school methods that are still effective. However, we cannot stress enough the importance of having a web presence.

Whenever you do undertake the development of your business website, we recommend the following:

Your website design should include your business name, logo, and slogan. The design elements, fonts, colors, letter styles of your website should mirror those of your advertising and marketing material wherever possible.

Your website should convey the same who, what, when, where, why, and how of your business as your business brochure.

It should provide links to the various platforms where your customers can make request, register complaints, schedule projects, or make payments.

Key personnel should be listed along with their respective job titles and email addresses.

5. Business Signage

Perhaps you have a service vehicle such as a van or truck. Having a sign painted on the vehicle or a magnetic sign stuck to the side of vehicle is a great way to advertise your business. Please keep in mind the following when creating your signage:

Uniformity. Like all your other advertising and marketing material, all signage designs should include your company name, logo, and slogan. In addition, your physical address, phone, email, website, etc., should be prominent. All information should be presented in big and bold copy so it will jump out and catch the eye of potential customers.

Signage should tell your potential customers what services you offer, i.e., maid service, special events, etc. Services should be displayed utilizing bold bullet points in the layout. Example: * *Maid Service* or * *Special Events*.

Finding and Reaching Customers

When deciding on your market and in conducting your market research, you should have identified who your potential customers are. Whether it's general contractors in the construction industry or everyday homeowners for your maid service, you are now task with getting your company's information into their hands and selling them on the idea of hiring you to provide them service.

There are several ways to go about achieving this objective—some are inexpensive and only require time and effort, while other require an investment of capital. We recommend you employ a mix of methods and, if at all possible, try to saturate the market with as much advertising and marketing material as possible. You want to get your name out into the marketplace so potential customers can become familiar with your brand. The methods we recommend are as follows:

RECESSION PROOF INCOME CLEANING UP IN THE COMMERCIAL OFFICE CLEANING BUSINESS

1. Cold Calling

Perhaps the least expensive method for getting information out about your company and into the hands of potential customers in by cold calling. Cold calling is simply picking up the phone and calling potential customers and pitching your service. This method can be highly effective. You never know when the decision maker is in need of your services. Your timing may be such that he just completed a project and is now in need of your services, or his existing service provider failed to show up. Please consider the following before making your first phone calls:

Build a contact database of potential customers to include the company name, address, telephone number, fax number, email address, and website. If you can, identify the person within the company who makes decision about your services. This is usually a purchasing agent in large corporation, and in most small businesses, it will probably be the businessowner themselves.

Write a script to work from when talking to potential customers. A script is simply a preplanned conversation about your business and the services you provide. Introduce yourself and your company, and clearly state the reason for your call (to provide information about your company and services). Don't be nervous, rigid, or afraid. Be flexible and ready to answer any questions. Be confident, know and believe in your business.

If possible, try to make an appointment to meet face-to-face, so you can provide additional information. This approach gives a personal touch to your marketing and sales efforts by allowing the decision maker to put a face to a company name. If not possible to meet face-to-face, find out if you can email the information or snail mail it to them. Whatever you do, make sure you do not terminate the conversation without having a method for getting your company's information into their hands.

Follow-up. Businesspeople are busy people, information often gets set aside or forgotten. Use good judgment in planning your follow-up calls. Don't become a nuisance. Allow ample time for the decision maker to receive your information and consider it. Every thirty days is a good benchmark.

2. Letter Writing

Often overlooked in the modern business climate, letter writing is an inexpensive and highly efficient method for getting your marketing material in front your potential customers. Decision makers do not always take cold calls or open unsolicited emails, but most everyone opens mail personally addressed to them. This method can be particularly useful if you are too shy or too busy to talk on the phone or meet face-to-face. However, it can be used simply because it works and is very effective.

By using your contact database of potential customers, you can write a letter introducing your company and the services you offer. Included in the information packet should be a copy of company's marketing brochure and your personal business card. The letter should be brief and end with an offer to speak further about your services at their convenience.

3. Bidders List and RFPs

Most major corporations and governments (local, state, and federal) use bidder list to prequalify potential service providers. To find out how to be added to a company's or agency's bidder list can be as simple as making a request either by phone, by letter, or visiting their website.

Many corporations and government agencies have a process that usually involves providing business documentation detailing your capabilities and/or certifying you are either a minority business enterprise (MBE), woman business enterprise (WBE), or a small business enterprise (SBE). There other certification types; however, these are the most common.

Once you have provided the required information and are approved, your company is added to a list of approved bidders. Whenever the company or government agency needs your services, they will either call you and asks you for a bid or proposal, or they will publish what is called a "Request for Proposals" (RFP) in the local newspaper or other legally mandated publication, such as the *Federal Register* so that interested prequalified bidders can submit a bid.

Becoming a certified prequalified bidder has many advantages and is well worth the effort. However, the process can be time-consuming and complicated. If you have the money, there are companies available that will help you navigate the certification process for a nominal fee.

4. Listing Services

Another way of finding and reaching potential customers is by registering your company with a Listing Service, such as Angie's List, Home Advisor, the Yellow Pages, or the Blue Book (construction-industry publication). With the exception of the Yellow Pages and the Blue Book, listing services operate like prequalified bidder's list. For a fee, they will list your company with their service. Whenever their subscribers or the general public needs someone to provide the services you offer, they can select from a list of names.

These services usually rank their member companies based on customer ratings. This can be either good or bad for your business, depending on the quality of your work or the fairness of the reviewer. Be careful. Your business reputation is worth its weight in gold. Once it is damaged or lost, it is difficult, if not impossible, to recover.

If you are going to pay to list your company with a service, we recommend those that do not have rating systems, such as the Yellow Pages or industry-specific publications like the Blue Book. In addition, no matter what listing service you use, we recommend you keep track of the number of referrals you are receiving and the amount of profits being generated because the success of your company is somewhat dependent upon how well they successfully market theirs.

5. Door-To-Door Sales

Like the name implies, this marketing method requires that you to do some footwork. Particularly, if your market concentration is on providing residential cleaning (maid) services. Leaving a brochure or flyer on a potential customer's doorstep can be highly effective. If you are working in a neighborhood, it is not a bad idea to take a few minutes before leaving to knock on a few doors and hand out a few flyers or brochures.

You should have a script ready so you are prepared to pitch your services with confidence. Look potential customers in the eye and state your purpose for being on their doorstep. Do not be forceful and try to pressure potential customers into talking. If they are busy or do not want to talk, just ask them if you can leave a brochure or flyer and then leave respectfully.

6. Subcontracting

If you don't mind splitting your profits or paying a finder's fee, this can be an excellent method for finding customers and building your business. As a start-up company, you may not have the time, money, or business savvy to generate leads and find customers. Companies like Jani-King are in the business of providing franchising or subcontracting opportunities for small start-up companies. They provide the customers. They do all advertising, marketing, and sales. You simply perform the work.

Jani-King and other companies like them usually require you to enter into a contractual relationship for a specific period of time. At the end of the contract period, Jani-King turns over the contract, and the customer becomes yours. This is a safe and proven method for finding customers and building a successful business.

7. Association Memberships

A great way to network and meet potential customers is to join industry associations and attend their conferences and events. If

RECESSION PROOF INCOME CLEANING UP IN THE COMMERCIAL OFFICE CLEANING BUSINESS

resources permit, you might even consider becoming a sponsor for one of their many events. Most industries have associations. They serve to keep member companies apprised of all issues affecting their industry, from changes in the legal and regulatory environment to the latest best practices for their industry. Have plenty of business cards on hand when attending conferences and events and take every opportunity to promote your company.

RECESSION-PROOF INCOME CREATION UP IN THE COMMERCIAL OFFICE CLEANING BUSINESS

Conclusion

Two fundamental qualities of the successful businessowner are drive and determination. By reaching the end of this book, you have demonstrated both of those qualities. In business, as well as in life, you will face many challenges, and having the commitment to see things through to the end will be invaluable to your success.

In this book, we set out to provide concrete steps to help you get your commercial office cleaning business up and running quickly. It is our hope that the real-world business experiences highlighted in this book have aided you to that end. It is certain that an academic background in business would be a valuable asset for the new businessowner, and we highly recommend you seek out and study business fundamentals.

However, before there were business books and an academic approach to conducting business, people just simply did. We are not discounting the value of academia; however, the suggestions contained in this book are proven. And if they worked for me, they are certain to work for you. Good luck in your business endeavor.

Douglas

Appendices

Case Studies

1. Nothing in My Hands or up My Sleeves

When I first started my business, I was eager to start bringing in customers and making money. Because of my experience as a purchasing agent, I began reaching out to other general contractors and offering my services. In addition, wherever I went, and whenever I was standing in line at the grocery store or around town, I would strike up a conversation with the person in front of me and begin pitching my services.

It wasn't until someone ask me for some information on my company that I realized I had been talking a good game but didn't have anything in the actual way of concrete marketing materials that would tell my potential customers who I was or what services I was offering. No business cards, no brochures, no nothing. I had absolutely nothing to give them when they hung up the phone or walked away.

I immediately stopped all my attempts at bringing in customers and focused on developing some materials for marketing my services. I already had my company name, the only thing left was to come up with a logo, craft a memorable slogan, and write a concrete description of my business so potential customers would not only know who I was and what services I was offering, but also know where I provided services, when I was available, why they should use my services over the competition, and how they could reach me.

Long on imagination but short on cash, I had a friend sketch an image of a man dressed in coveralls and running a buffer. That became my logo. To make my company stand out from the crowd, I developed a slogan that would evoke an image of quality, professionalism, and demand. "Your cleaning contractor of choice" became my slogan.

Finally, I began drafting the who, what, when, where, why, and how of my company for use in my brochures, on flyers, and the website I developed using Microsoft FrontPage. Using my laser printer, I had the image and slogan printed on stationary and business cards, using quality paper I purchased from Staples. With a digital copy, I was able to transfer the icon and slogan onto brochures and flyers that would eventually find their way into the hands of my potential customers.

Through this experience, I learned the importance of keeping marketing materials on hand at all times and how to utilize the resources I had at my disposal to accomplish my business goals. I was able to draw on the talents of a friend and use the skills and knowledge I had acquired through real-world business workplace experience.

2. Business Focus—Narrowing My Services

When I started my business, I tried to do everything, maid service, janitorial services, day porters, etc. My ad in the Yellow Pages highlighted all my service offerings with bold bullet points. Eventually, the phone started ringing, and I was soon going to companies, doing a walk-through of their facility, and providing quotes.

One day, as I was leaving a walk-through, I noticed there was some construction going on in the building next door. Since my business experience was in construction, I decided to walk over and talk to the project manager. After a short while, we began to talk about his upcoming need for someone to provide the final cleaning (*the cleaning provided before turning the completed project over to the owner*) on the project. I gave him my card, a business brochure, and I left. About a month later, I got a call from that project manager, asking me to come by and give him a quote on the final cleaning.

From that experience, I immediately realized that opportunities in construction final cleaning could be capitalized on by going from project-to-project and talking with project managers about their needs. Since I had real-world experience as a purchasing agent and writing construction final cleaning contracts, I decided to focus on developing my primary expertise in the construction final cleaning market.

I started a subscription to Construction Market Data (www.cmdgroup.com) and began to identify construction projects in the region that were nearing completion and would soon have a need for my services. Whenever, I would go to talk to a project manager, I would look around for other projects ongoing in the area and stop and talk with the project managers, leaving a business card and brochure.

Because most construction companies have more than one project ongoing, my business began to grow exponentially. I was soon getting calls from other project managers within the various companies and doing construction final cleaning projects exclusively all over the Baltimore–Washington region.

By concentrating my marketing efforts in an area I knew best, construction final cleaning, I was able to leverage my previous work experience into a successful foundation for my new business. Through this experience I learned the value of having market knowledge and the profound difference a personal touch can make simply by talking to a potential customer face-to-face.

3. Bread and Butter

Every businessowner dreams of having a steady stream of uninterrupted income. Some businessowners believe that having a single, large, high-dollar company as a customer is the ultimate bread and butter for their business. It almost means certain business success. Finding a high-value customer who utilizes your services exclusively can be a dream come true. However, it can also be a company's worst nightmare and, potentially, lead to their eventual demise.

As my company began to get referrals from other project managers within the same construction company, I stayed busy. The work was steady, and the money was great. At one point, I was making more than 75 percent of my profits from the one company. I slowed down chasing work with other contractors and narrowed my market concentration, just so I could satisfy the needs of this one client.

Nearly all my company's resources (labor, equipment, and supplies) were constantly tied up in providing services to their projects. I eventually had to start turning down work in order to fulfill my commitments to this one customer. This decision turned out to be one of my biggest mistakes as a new businessowner and proved to be near fatal to my business.

After some time, the construction industry slowed down, and the number of projects became fewer and fewer. The projects I did get were small-tenant renovations and paid low dollars. To top it all off, the contractor began to take his time in paying me for my services. I would have to wait well beyond the standard thirty days before seeing a dime.

This made it difficult for me to pay employees or purchase materials and supplies. I had to let some employees go and was severely limited as to the number of projects I could bid on from other contractors, and because I had stopped chasing work with them, I had no reputation or working relationship from which to leverage business.

Fortunately, I was able to ride out the downturn in the construction final cleaning business and was eventually able to fill the void left by the lull in business from my bread and butter customer. I had to use my business savings and develop business relationships in other commercial office cleaning market segments—i.e., barbershops, doctor's offices, and maid services.

We all know the importance of eating a well-balanced meal. Through this experience, I learned that the success of a business is no different. The long-term success of a business depends on it receiving nourishment from many different sources. For me, this meant that if I was to remain in business, in addition to having reserve profits (savings), I would have to develop and maintain a broad array of customers across multiple-market segments.

Business Communication (Examples)

Business Introduction Letter

My Cleaning Company
2345 Maple Ave.
Anywhere, USA XXXXX-2345
(XXX) XXX-XXXX

January 1, 20xx
Mr. John Doe
General Offices, Inc.
123 Main Ave.
Anywhere, USA xxxxx-123

Dear Mr. Doe:

    My name is _____, and I am writing to introduce you to our company. We are a new commercial office cleaning business that is now offering services in your area. We provide a complete range of custodial and janitorial services, to include day porters, night janitors, and optional services for special weekend events. I have enclosed for your information and consideration a brochure detailing who we are and why you should consider us for all your present and future office cleaning needs.

Should you have any questions or would like to discuss your immediate needs, you may reach me at (xxx-xxx-xxxx) or by visiting our website at www.mycleaningcompany.com.

Sincerely,

Douglas Smith
Owner

Encl:

Cold Calling Script

(Actual Person on the Line)

To the receptionist answering. Hello, my name is _____, and I am calling from XZY Company. And I would like to speak with the person responsible for deciding on your office cleaning/janitorial needs.

To the decision maker. Hello, Mr./Mrs. _____, my name is _____, and the reason for my call is to introduce you to our company and the services we provide. And if you have the time, I would like to discuss your current needs and how we can help.

Scenario 1. If the person is busy, find out if you can follow-up with an email or letter providing the who, what, when, where, how, and why of your business. Be sure to get their name, title, direct phone number, and email address for your contact database.

Scenario 2. If they have time to talk, discuss with them the who, what, when, where, how, and why of your company and find out if they are happy with their current service provider or if they currently have a need. If they are happy with their current service, ask if you can send them some information about your company by email or letter, and if it is okay to check back with them periodically to assess their needs or apprise them of new service offerings.

Scenario 3. If they have a current need and are interested in your services, set an appointment for as soon as possible so you can talk face-to-face and close the deal. Don't forget to bring business cards and marketing materials.

(Voicemail)

To the decision maker. Hello, my name is _____, and I am calling from XZY Company. The reason I am calling is to introduce you to our company and the services we provide. At your convenience, I would like to discuss your current office cleaning/janitorial needs. You may reach me at (xxx-xxx-xxxx) or by visiting our website at www.mycleaningcompany.com for more information. Thank you and I look forward to speaking with you. Goodbye.

Business Proposal

My Cleaning Company
2345 Maple Ave.
ANYWHERE, USA XXXXX-2345
(XXX) XXX-XXXX

January 1, 20xx
Mr. John Doe
General Offices, Inc.
123 Main Ave.
Anywhere, USA xxxxx-123

Dear Mr. Doe:

Our proposal is to furnish all labor, material, and equipment necessary to provide complete custodial services to your facility located at 123 Main Ave. in Anywhere, USA, for the monthly price of $1,200. All services will be provided Monday to Friday, and the scope of our work include the following:

Vacuum all carpet floors;

Sweep and mop all tile floors;

Dust all surfaces; to include book shelves, ceiling fans, desk, and window blinds;

Clean and sanitize all bathrooms;

Fill all bathroom hand soap dispensers;

Supply all toilet paper;

Clean and sanitize the kitchenette;

Fill kitchenette hand soap dispenser; and

Empty all trash cans and recyclable comingles (glass, cans, and paper).

Please note that this proposal is valid for sixty (60) days.

Should you have any questions or wish to discuss this proposal in further detail, please contact me at your convenience.

Sincerely,

Douglas A. Smith
Owner

Resource Guide

www.sba.gov. US Small Business Administration is an excellent resource for everything small business.

www.inbia.org. The National Business Incubation Association is an organization geared toward speeding up the growth and success of startup and early stage companies. They're often a good path to capital from angel investors, state governments, economic-development coalitions, and other investors. Their website has a search engine where you can locate a business incubator near you.

www.irs.gov. Everything tax related. Excellent advice on what forms and documents are needed for start-up and ongoing business operations.

www.aicpa.org. American Institute of CPAs (certified public accountants) provides assistance in locating and verifying qualified CPAs across the US.

www.thebalancesmb.com. Website with links to the secretary of state for all fifty US states. The secretary of state is responsible for registering and licensing businesses for that particular state. Your secretary of state's website will be a great source for obtaining start-up information and getting a line on the competition.

www.softwareconnect.com. The website where you can evaluate the most widely used small business accounting software on the market today.

www.entrepreneur.com. Excellent article discussing what is branding and why it is important for your business.

www.impakter.com. Using color in building your brand, how to use color to persuade.

www.squarespace.com. Excellent resource for building your website or finding a web developer.

www.top5-crm.com. Excellent resource for evaluating customer relations management software, i.e., contact databases.

www.prodpx-promotool.usps.com. US Postal Service has direct mail information and services.

www.usa.gov/government-contracting-for-beginners. This website offers a primer of how to begin contracting with the federal government. You may find the process or the business information requirements similar for most state and local government agencies, as well as major corporations.

www.angieslistbusinesscenter.com. Angie's List is a business referral service.

www.homeadvisor.com. Home Advisor is a business referral service.

http://www.thebluebook.com. The Blue Book is a building and construction listing service for construction final cleaning and large office building cleaning.

www.cmdgroup.com. Construction Market Data is an excellent resource for obtaining leads on construction projects.

www.janiking.com. Contains franchising and subcontracting information and opportunities.

www.boma.org. Building Owners and Managers Association has marketing contacts, trade education, etc.

About the Author

The youngest of five children, Douglas Smith grew up in rural West Virginia, where he was raised by a divorced mother, who cleaned houses during the day and studied nursing at night. As a child, he would help his mother clean houses by sweeping and dusting, while she performed the more detailed house cleaning chores. When he became a teen, he began cleaning doctor's offices and washing dishes at a local restaurant to earn money.

Upon graduating high school, Smith entered college, where he studied political science and legal studies. In addition to this traditional education, he holds certificates in accounting and computer programming and operations. In the years before becoming a businessowner, Smith worked in a variety of business support positions, to include bank clerk, computer operations supervisor, purchasing agent, small/disadvantaged business certification specialist, and legal/regulatory assistant.

Smith credits the work ethic instilled in him in his early life and his broad work experiences in diverse business sectors as factors in helping him achieve personal success as a businessowner. Semi-retired, Smith advises young start-ups, and in his spare time, he enjoys reading, writing, playing the guitar, and studying martial arts.

www.ingramcontent.com/pod-product-compliance
Lightning Source LLC
Chambersburg PA
CBHW021037180526
45163CB00005B/2170